Folk an Ethnonationalism Explained

Arthur Kemp B.A. (Pol. Sci., Intl. Pol., Pub. Admin.)

Ostara Publications

Folk and Nation—Ethnonationalism Explained

By Arthur Kemp

First published 2008

Reprinted 2009, 2010, 2011

This edition 2012

Ostara Publications

www.ostarapublications.com

ISBN 978-1-291-16616-3

Contents

Other books by Arthur Kemp

March of the Titans, The Complete History of the White Race

The Immigration Invasion: How Third World Immigration is Destroying the First World and What Must be Done to Stop It

Jihad: Islam's 1,300 Year War on Western Civilization

Four Flags: The Indigenous People of Great Britain

The Children of Ra: Artitistic, Historical and Genetic Evidence for Ancient White Egypt

The Lie of Apartheid and Other True Stories from Southern Africa

Victory or Violence: The Story of the AWB of South Africa

All available from www.ostarapublications.com

Introduction

This booklet first saw the light of day in 2008 as an internal training work for a nationalist party in Britain. As such, it has a heavy accent on the UK. The booklet's popularity made it clear, however, that it warranted a more widely available version.

The text of this version has been only slightly changed from the original training booklet, in that specific references to parties have been removed.

This makes it more universal, and the ideas contained therein can now be used as a manual to propagate the idea of ethnonationalism—among all peoples across the world.

The idea of ethnonationalism stands in direct contrast to the "one-world" designs of present-day internationalist elites. As such, it represents a truly revolutionary—and, from the internationalist point of view, dangerous—idea. If the various peoples of the world, European, Asian, African and Amerind, all decide that preserving their on individual identities is more important than the "global melting pot," a new dawn will have arisen.

Contrary to what is propagated by the Internationalists, the ideology of ethnonationalism is the true champion of diversity. For what is diversity except the appreciation and nurturing of individual identities?

And what better way to nurture and protect individual identities than by preserving them, free from oppression and exploitation, and submersion in an internationalist elite?

The internationalists, who seek to destroy national identities, who seek to submerge races and force everyone into a uniform, identical mass, are in fact the true enemies of diversity.

For, left to run its course, internationalism will ultimately lead to the destruction of individual identities, races, cultures and will eventually wipe out the wonderful human diversity with which Mother Nature blessed this earth.

Ethnonationalism—or the demand of ethnically distinct peoples to rule themselves in their own geographic areas—provides the only real answer to the Internationalist nightmare.

May this work serve as ammunition to all people of goodwill of all races, to increase their demand for self-determination, freedom, mutual respect, and appreciation for diversity. In that ideal, lies our collective hope for survival.

Arthur Kemp, October 2012.

1. Ethnonationalism – A definition

Ethnic nationalism is nationalism wherein the 'nation' is defined in terms of ethnicity.

Whatever specific ethnicity is involved, ethnic nationalism always includes some element of descent from previous generations.

It also includes ideas of a culture shared between members of the group, and with their ancestors, and usually a shared language.

This concept stands in direct contrast to the universality promoted by the Left, and to the civic nationalism promoted by the Right, and to the hybrid of the two used by global capitalism to justify exploitation *sans frontiers*.

The Left generally decry any form of nationalism, with its extremes often seeking to totally destroy any borders or specific identity in favour of a utopian borderless society of the world; whereas civic nationalism argues that, although there are defined national identities, anyone, from anywhere on the globe, can join a nation simply by 'cultural assimilation'.

This view argues that once someone has learned the language, they become members of that nation. Of course, the concept of ethno-nationalism rejects both these views as invalid.

2. Central Tenets of Ethnonationalism

There are a number of central tenets to the concept of ethnonationalism.

These are:

2.1 Each ethnic group on earth is entitled to self-determination.

In other words, each and every group has the right to rule themselves, for better or for worse, in their own territories.

The right to self-determination is enshrined in the founding charter of the United Nations, and has a well-established international legal precedent behind it, as well as a centuries'- old history in the mainstream of Western political philosophy.

2.2 Ethnic nationalism bases membership of the nation on descent or heredity, rather than on political membership. Once again this is an old legal concept as well, known as jus sanguinis (the law of blood).

In other words, ethnic nationalism defines a nation by its original founding people, within a defined geographic territory.

2.3 An ethno-nationalist state derives political legitimacy from its status as homeland of that ethnic group, from its protective function against colonisation, persecution or racism, and from its purpose to provide a communal cultural and social life, which is not possible under the 'borderless society' or the civic nationalist models.

3. Underlying concepts of Ethnonationalism

3.1 Race

Race is a biological reality, despite nearly 100 years of arguments to the contrary. However, as outlined below, the concept of race has been subjected to abuse by extremists, from all sides of the political spectrum and thus remains one of the most controversial subjects with which to deal.

A race is defined as a group of people who share visible – and non-visible – common characteristics.

The visible characteristics include skin colour, facial features, hair texture, and in many cases, stature; while the non-visible characteristics are those things which give rise to the visible, namely differences in genetic make-up.

It is vital, when discussing the concept of race, that all notions of alleged 'superiority' and 'inferiority' are disregarded and cast aside.

All peoples, all races, have a right to equal dignity and respect, and it is morally incorrect to regard any individual as 'inferior' simply because of their racial origin. Any policy position or argument using that premise is morally bankrupt as well as politically 'unsellable'.

It is in no way disparaging to talk about the concept of race.

Advances in the study of genetics have now conclusively disproved the leftist argument that "race is a social construct." The vast differences in DNA structure – which are so far-reaching that even race-specific medicines are being developed to address race-specific illnesses – have shown that race is a valid, scientific taxonomic concept.

Indeed, the more that is discovered about race-specific illnesses, the clearer it becomes that the liberal-left 'race deniers', far from doing some kind of service to humanity, in fact condemn many members of non- European races to unnecessary debilitating diseases and premature death. Realism in this subject benefits everybody.

The controversy over the concept of race has always been on the subject of cognitive abilities, linked to racist arguments. This **5** subject does, however, not enter the arguments for an ethnonationalist state, because even if there were no differences at all, the argument for ethno-nationalism remains utterly untouched or affected, and is as valid as ever.

To summarise:

3.1.1 Race is defined as a group of people who share common physical, cultural and hereditary factors;

3.1.2 Modern DNA has proven beyond any question that race is a valid taxonomic concept;

3.1.3 A discussion of race must be divorced from racist arguments over alleged 'superiority' or 'inferiority' as the validity – or otherwise – of the arguments have no effect whatsoever on the validity of the argument for an ethno-nationalist state.

3.2 Ethnicity

Ethnicity is the name given to the cultural expression of a defined group of people. This can be a shared language, culture, religion, interests or any other socially created common characteristic.

In essence then, ethnicity can be taken to mean an individual's hereditary and cultural origin, and not that person's place of birth (as the civic nationalists try to argue).

A few examples will suffice: Chinese in Britain will refer to themselves as 'Chinese British', blacks will refer to themselves as 'Black British' and even create organisations devoted to promoting their racial and ethnic interests (such as the formally recognised National Black Police Officers' Federation, and so on).

By way of underlining this point, many notable British individuals, born overseas, are not regarded as anything but ethnically British, despite the place of their birth.

Two simple-to-quote examples include the actress Joanna Lumley (born in India) and the comedian Spike Milligan (born in India to an Irish father). No one seriously claims that either of these two individuals are actually Indians, despite being born on that subcontinent.

3.3 Territory

One of the most important pillars upon which the ethno-nationalist state stands is the concept of territory. In fact, a defined territory is vital for the development of an ethnic group, for without a territory, a sense of unity and belonging, based upon the initial bond of heredity, cannot develop.

In this way, an English identity, a Scottish identity, a Welsh identity, an Irish identity, a Chinese identity, a Japanese identity, an Australian Aboriginal identity, an Indian identity, a Kikuyu identity (Kenya), and so on, have all developed because of the common bond of territory between individuals who already share a common hereditary bond.

Proof of the validity of this concept is the historical fact of conflict between different ethnic groups either trying to share, or to dominate, a territory with other ethnic groups.

This is the cause of much of the troubled history of national wars in Europe, and of what is loosely called ethnic or tribal conflict in other countries, such as Darfur in the Sudan (where Arabs and blacks are at each others' throats) or Rwanda (where two tribes, the Hutu and the Tutsi, are in conflict).

Once again, the concept of a defined territory as belonging to a particular ethnic group carries with it no racist connotations at all.

It could even be argued that colonial racism, which saw European colonial powers grab as much territory as possible, without due regard for traditional territorial divisions between ethnicities in Africa, is the cause of much conflict today.

The states created artificially by colonialism, comprising a host of different ethnicities (such as the Rwandan example given above), have laid the basis for numerous civil wars in the Third World.

Without colonialism, it could be argued, these ethnic groups would have likely developed into their own nation states, quite distinct from the other ethnic groups – with whom they now **7** share disputed territory as a result of the colonialist experiment.

In other words, much inter-ethnic conflict in the Third World could have been avoided, had the colonial powers not ignored the imperative of territory and the reality of human territoriality in the formation of national states.

4. The Implications of Ethnonationalism

The implications of ethno-nationalism are therefore profound.

These implications are:

1. All ethnic groups have a right to be themselves in their own territories;

2. All ethnic groups have a right to retain their own traditions, culture, heritage and identity, without fear of being overwhelmed, threatened or dominated by any other group;

3. The demand for self-determination must be granted equally, fairly and without favour or prejudice to all peoples on earth;

4. Each ethnic group has the right to maintain their own territories for their own people to ensure that their culture, heritage, tradition and identity remain intact.

5. Any intention, move, action or threat by any other ethnic group, to take over and occupy, by military means or otherwise, is an intrusion upon the rights of the subject ethnic group.

6. Ethno-nationalism does not rely on subjective arguments of racial 'superiority' or 'inferiority' – all ethnic groups must be free to rule themselves as they alone see fit, and cannot claim any special status simply on account of their hereditary origin.

This applies to ALL ethnic groups: European, African, Asian, Aboriginal or American Indian.

5. The Practical Application of Ethnonationalism

5.1 Population In terms of practical application with regard to the British Isles, this means accepting the scientific fact, proven by recent DNA studies, that the majority of indigenous people who live in Britain are descendants of those who either moved here at the end of the last Ice Age, or in 'later' Neolithic times. They have maintained an almost continuous heredity line, absorbing only minor amounts of immigrants, mainly from neighbouring European nations, and have the right to protect and defend themselves from military invasion (such as the threat posed by World War II) or from mass immigration.

5.2 Economics Ethno-nationalism also implies an understanding that each ethnic group has the right to protect its own economy, and not be subjected to the dictates of international corporations, job outsourcing and the destruction of that nation's industrial or manufacturing capacity. This will be dealt with in full in another booklet.

5.3 Social Ordering Ethno-nationalism also implies that each ethnic group has a primary responsibility to its own people first, and only thereafter, if the spare capacity exists, to help others.

This means, for example, that the legitimate demands of foreign aid should be subject to the demands of the needs of the ethnic group from whom the finance (taxes) were raised in the first place. Only once there are no British people in need, can consideration be given to foreign aid. Charity does indeed begin at home for the ethno-nationalist.

5.4 Education Ethno-nationalism also implies that an ethnic group has the right to generate its own educational standards, which produce material which will engender pride, a sense of belonging and identity, and ethnic consciousness, within that ethnic group.

Under no circumstances should any ethnic group be forced to subject its children to an educational system designed to alienate them from their ethnic identity.

6. Attacks on Ethnonationalism

Attacks on the concept of ethno-nationalism have two origins: firstly, historical factors, and secondly, the use of incorrect, sometimes even factually wrong, arguments by those proposing the ethno-nationalist ideal.

6.1 Historical Causes

The cause of ethno-nationalism has been partly harmed by historical factors, in particular the obsession with 1930s Germany.

It is important to consider, at this juncture, that the concept of ethno-nationalism is as old as history itself, and did not originate in any 20th Century country. In fact, the development of Europe into nation-states is the product of ethno-nationalism. World War I was the result of European countries ignoring the concept of ethno-nationalism and trying to incorporate different ethnicities into one state (the Austro- Hungarian Empire in particular).

In reality, the concept of ethnonationalism is not unique to any one particular country or ideological movement. Nazi Germany was certainly a pro-German (and even Germanic) movement, but then so is Zionism, which is merely Jewish ethnonationalism.

Opposition to ethnonationalism based on "smears" from the past at increasingly unbelievable as more and more people of different races and geographic areas demand the right to self-determination. There is no reason for any ehtnonationalist to bow down before such attacks, and only to point out the above—and then move on to propagating the concept, rather than getting bogged down in trying to defend it against baseless smears.

6.2 The Use of Incorrect Arguments

Advocates of ethno-nationalism have also erred in the past in the way they have presented their arguments to the general public. In a nutshell, they have played into the enemy's hands by adhering to the 'stereotype racist' idea that the mass media, in particular, has managed to implant in the population's psyche.

Before presenting a list of incorrect arguments, it is well worth considering that many of these arguments are not watertight, but, even if they were, they still have no bearing, positive or negative, on the case for ethno-nationalism, as outlined above.

6.2.1 Race and IQ

Virtually every scientific study on the topic has indicated that there is a group differential gap between the various broad racial groups.

For years, this gap has been used to argue the 'superiority' of Europeans. The most widely publicised book on the topic remains the New York Times bestseller, *The Bell Curve,* written by Richard J. Herrnstein and Charles Murray. (Herrnstein was Jewish, which somewhat defeated the argument that the book was 'Nazi'.) Those advocating white supremacy often use this book to justify their beliefs, citing the average 20 point gap between blacks and whites. However, people using this argument have most likely never actually read the whole book, because if they had, they would have seen that certain groups of South East Asians have on average four to five point higher IQ levels than whites.

A white supremacist argument based on IQ is self-contradictory, because according to that logic, the most 'intelligent' race –certain groups of Asians—should be top of the racial totem pole (in that worldview, at least).

Also, basing an argument for an ethno-state upon 'IQ superiority' will always be bedevilled by the genuine existence of highly intelligent individuals of non-European origin, who can be used to easily defeat an IQ-based argument. ("Here is Dr Obanga, the world famous heart surgeon from Guys Hospital in London, are you saying he has an IQ of 80?" and so on.)

As valid scientifically as they may be, the truth is that ultimately, IQ differences make absolutely no difference to the argument in favour of ethno-nationalism.

Even if every group were identical, or, as is the case, certain Asian groups have the highest IQs, none of that would diminish the right of any ethnic group to self-determination in its own territory.

6.3 Racist Jargon

The use of racist jargon or epithets is yet another way of allowing the enemy to reinforce the idea of 'racist' as being identical to ethno-nationalism. Activists must under all circumstances, in private and in public, avoid such language.

It is always possible to present arguments in favour of ethno-nationalism with civility and respect for all races and ethnicities.

7. How to Argue the Case for Ethno-Nationalism

Contrary to what many may think, it is a simple task to argue the case for an ethno-nationalist state without giving offence to any person or group, by just following a basic line of thought which leads the listener to no other conclusion except to agree that the proponent 'has a point' and is correct.

Activists are encouraged to develop their own version of the following argument: Each ethnic group has developed its own culture and civilisation in its own geographic area - ethno-nationalism in action - and each and every ethnic group is entitled to due respect. It is possible to always talk in objective terms about each nation's civilisation.

We can therefore talk, without fear of offence, of a Chinese civilisation, a Japanese civilisation, a Zulu civilisation, an Indian civilisation, and, of course, a British civilisation, all in objective terms.

Each of these civilisations has arisen, mostly independently, in distinct territories. In fact, a society or civilisation is only a reflection of the population of that particular territory.

For example, the Chinese civilisation is a product of the Chinese people, and is a reflection of the make-up of the population living in China. The Chinese civilisation is unique to the Chinese people; they made it and it reflects their values and norms.

As the Chinese people made the Chinese civilisation, it logically follows that the Chinese culture would disappear if the Chinese people were to disappear.

Presently the overwhelming majority of Chinese people live in China, creating the Chinese civilisation in that land. If, however, Australian Aborigines were to immigrate into China in their millions, and the Chinese population had to dramatically reduce in number, then in a few years the character of Chinese civilisation would change - to reflect the new inhabitants of that territory.

In other words, the society or civilisation of that territory would then reflect the fact that the majority of inhabitants were now Australian Aborigines rather than Chinese people. If China had to fill up with Aborigines, this would mean the end of Chinese civilisation. Aborigines would create a new civilisation which would reflect themselves, and not that of the Chinese people.

If all Chinese people on earth had to disappear tomorrow, then fairly obviously, Chinese civilisation and culture would disappear with them.

That this should be the case is actually perfectly logical. It is has nothing to do with which culture is more advanced, or any notions of superiority or inferiority. It is merely a reflection of the fact that a civilisation is a product of the nature of the people making up the population in the territory.

It is this obvious principle which determines the creation and dissolution of cultures and identities: once the people who create a certain culture or identity disappear, then that culture and identity will disappear with them.

If the vanished population is replaced by different peoples, then a new society or culture is created, which reflects the new inhabitants of that region.

There are numerous examples of this process at work. One which will be familiar to all is the shift which occurred in North America. On that continent, the American Indian people lived for thousands of years, creating a way of life which dominated that continent.

In other words, the culture which dominated North America reflected the fact that the American Indian people lived and formed the majority population there.

After 1500 AD, however, that continent filled up with white immigrants from Europe. These white immigrants displaced the Amerinds by squeezing them out of possession of North America.

The great shift in North American civilisation then occurred.

Whereas the Amerind culture had dominated for thousands of **18** years, within a couple hundred years the dominant civilisation on that continent had become white European.

This shift reflected the fact that the majority of inhabitants of North America had become white Europeans - and the Amerind civilisation, for all practical purposes, disappeared. The Amerind civilisation in North America 'fell' because the population of North America changed.

In other words, mass immigration by Europeans to North America, effectively destroyed American Indian civilisation, by the population being replaced with new immigrants who did not share the common heritage, culture, traditions and identity of the American Indians.

In Britain, official projections are that within 50 years, mass immigration, combined with natural reproduction rates of immigrants already present, will mean that the ethnic British will be a minority in this country.

Unless the right of the British people to self-determination in an ethno-nationalist state is observed, the woeful fate of the American Indian awaits the native British.

This is not an 'extremist' demand. It is in fact one of the most moderate, reasonable, demand any nation can make, and one which is afforded to every Third World nation on earth – the right to be oneself in one's own territory.

If it were to be announced, for example, that Indians in India were going to become a minority and perhaps vanish altogether by the year 2100 due to European colonization, one can bet that there would be merry hell to play in the international media and the United Nations. It would be proclaimed as "genocide" and active Indian resistance to such "denial of their human rights" would be encouraged and supported—and rightly so.

Yet the demographics in European countries, North America, Australia and New Zealand are heading for precisely that scenario—with the only difference that it is the European peoples on the receiving end. The silence from the media and establishment is deafening.

The hypocrisy of the situation is something that is obvious and apparent to all but the willingly blind—and presents an ideal opportunity for the ethnonationalist argument.

8. Conclusion

There might be some who would claim that the idea of "ethno-nationalism" is impossible, outdated, or for some other reason, somehow unacceptable.

If this were so, then why, it could be asked, does the United Nations have a permanent forum dedicated to the rights of "indigenous peoples"?

Why would the Indians of the Amazonian rainforest demand protection for their culture and their heritage?

Why would the people of Tibet demand—and receive—international support and acclaim for their demand to be free of Chinese Han domination?

Why would the African people be praised for resisting European domination and rule?

Why would Canada grant territorial rights to the Inuit people in Nunavut and even create a separate territory for the indigenous people of that region? The territory of Nunavut is not some "ancient" or "outdated" creation—it was established on July 9, 1993, through the the Nunavut Land Claims Agreement Act and the Nunavut Act, both passed by the Canadian Parliament. The transition to establish Nunavut Territory was completed on April 1, 1999.

Why would the American government—which is supposedly totally committed to "internationalism" allow and support the continued existence of 310 Indian reservations in the continental United States, in which Europeans and other non-Indians are even forbidden from owning property?

Why would Western governments—without exception—support Israel, which has a specifically Jew-only immigration policy and even outlaws marriage between Jews and non-Jews?

Of course, all of the above-mentioned examples (and there are many more) have one important common factor: they are all non-European. It would seem that the Internationalists are prepared to (just) accept any assertion of ethnonationalism, as long as it is non-European in origin.

There is no justification for this double standard. The European people, and their individual nation states, have just as much right to self-determination as any other people on earth, and any person with even the slightest tinge of fair play and decency will acknowledge this to be true.

For if any of the above-mentioned peoples and races have the right to be free of outside rule, of forced integration, of enforced dissolution into a globalist mass, and have the right to assert their own culture in their own territories, then the European peoples and nation states have that exact same right.

Therein lies the most powerful argument for ethnonationalism: that it is not based on the demand to suppress, oppress, disadvantage, or rule anybody else, but rather upon the right to be free of all of those strictures.

It is a right which all ethnonationalists, of any creed, origin or race, will endorse and accept. It is reasonable, moral, and just.

Appendix 1: An Understanding of Group Behaviour

According to Professor Robert D. Putnam from Harvard University, in a famous paper called *E Pluribus Unum: Diversity and Community in the Twenty-first Century,* mass immigration is the primary cause of social disharmony.

According to Putnam, immigration and ethnic diversity tend to reduce social solidarity and social capital. Evidence from the United States of America shows, he says, that in ethnically diverse neighbourhoods residents of all races tend to 'hunker down'. Trust (even of one's own race) is lower, altruism and community cooperation rarer, friends fewer.

Belonging to an 'in-group' is one of the core human rights and needs. Identity politics is the trend of the modern world (see, for example, the growing number of nation-states throughout the last century) because it is natural and good – and reasonable.

It is a right which does not infringe upon the rights of any others, and is a right which is morally correct and can be defended on any platform.

It is in fact, the single most reasonable request which any nation or people can demand: the right to be themselves in their own territory.

So why does it seem to be such a struggle to persuade European peoples in particular to adhere to this basic principle?

The well-known American professor of psychology, Kevin McDonald, in an article in the journal The Occidental Quarterly, has addressed this very issue. McDonald's writing provides a fascinating – and intrinsically true – insight into White behavioural patterns.

Essentially, McDonald says that Whites have, through the evolutionary process, developed an extremely high degree of conscientiousness. This entails diligent application to work, day-to-day tasks and intellectual pursuits which have, without question, allowed Europeans to develop technology which is unsurpassed anywhere in the world.

This conscientiousness, has however, had a price, argues McDonald. The price for conscientiousness has been social and material advancement – not a bad thing in itself, but this had brought with it a large degree of social self-control.

All too often, social ostracism in European society has led to disastrous outcast status, which has directly affected the material advancement – and social standing – of those who are outcasts.

For a conscientious person, therefore, social ostracism leads to material loss, and loss of social standing – and both of these potential problems will severely affect the psychological well-being of a conscientious person.

Therefore, McDonald argues, European people, being the most conscientious, are subject to the greatest amount of pressure to conform.

Non-conformity leads to social ostracism, which in turn leads to potential financial loss and a lowering of social status. Both these are anathema to a conscientious person, never mind a conscientious group.

Ever since the Left won the political day, McDonald continues, it has become difficult to dissent from the prevailing opinion on race and immigration, without suffering the consequences of social ostracism, and the difficulties it generates.

This does not, however, mean that Europeans do not see or even do not understand what is going on. He quotes several American opinion polls which have found, for example, that over 70% of White Americans think it is worthwhile to preserve European civilisation, yet, they continue to vote for political leaders whose implicit and openly stated policies will lead to the destruction of that very civilization.

In Britain, opinion polls have consistently shown that the British public has always opposed both the EU Superstate and mass immigration. Yet, we also know that only a relatively few number of the British voting public actually vote for parties which support what the opinion polls say are the most popular prevailing opinions on the EU and immigration.

The bottom line – in both America and Britain – is this: Whites as a group, in opinion polls, endorse policies that will guarantee their survival, but when given political choices, they vote for politicians who are opposed to those policies.

McDonald explains this contradiction in terms of self-imposed censorship and screening, driven primarily by the urge to be conscientious and not face social ostracism. White people, he says, instinctively react negatively to their displacement by immigrants, but enforce learned self-control over their instinctive urges, in order to keep their social acceptance and not face social ostracism.

In this way, McDonald says, Whites start coalescing in groups which are overtly White, yet do not, as the learned professor says, "say the name."

In other words, Whites, especially the liberal ones, while paying lip service to integration and immigration, take steps to ensure that they themselves, and their children, are kept as far away as possible from the consequences of those policies.

They do this, McDonald says, not because they are not aware of what is going on, but only because they fear the social ostracism which might come with dissension from the prevailing political view on the topic.

This explains the phenomenon of "White Flight" from the cities, the formation of social interest groups which are overtly White in constituent parts (for example, in America, 'country music' or Nascar racing; in Britain 'country life'; 'Englishness", Scottishness. Welshness etc.)

All of these activities allow Whites to physically congregate in groups which are overwhelmingly European, yet do not use any mention of the word 'race.'

Everyone knows that the exodus from the cities, for example, by Whites is the direct result of those cities filling up with non-White immigrants. Everyone knows that the wealthy are removing their children from public schools where the non-White student ratio is too high, to private schools where wealth affords a measure of segregation – but no-one uses the 'race' word to explain it.

Instead, they will say it is 'for better education' or 'the country life' or 'a better place to raise children' and so on.

All this confirms the truth of McDonald's thesis: namely that Whites' conscious behaviour of being "anti-racist" is in direct contradiction to their overt behaviour.

Whites choose freely not to live in non-White areas, and will make superhuman efforts to get out, but will never admit that their reason for doing so was racial. This would lead to the much feared social ostracism.

White ethno-centricism is very real and alive, it just manifests itself in ways which cannot be identified as an overtly pro-White fashion.

McDonald concludes by saying that the way out of this problem is twofold: firstly, bold assertive announcements by individuals of pride in their racial and cultural heritage; and secondly, the creation of White associations where the Whiteness of that group is overt and regarded as the norm, rather than being cause for social exclusion.

This conclusion, as valid as it is, is not however the final answer on the matter. To address the very real fear Whites have with the word 'race', will require more than just the two solutions McDonald suggests.

The real issue is to tackle and identify those issues upon which the vast majority of the public feel strongly – immigration, economics etc. – in a fashion which will make them comfortable to be associated with, and not make them think they will give up their social status by being known publicly to support such policies.

Pronouncements on 'racial superiority' for example, are often counter-productive as they are largely subjective – everyone likes to think of themselves as better, and which group is better in an absolute sense can and does often turn into a very negative political debate which leads nowhere.

Arguments based on group IQ are similarly problematic. IQ-based arguments, while true for groups, are more difficult to assert on an individual level. Within any one individual's circle of acqaintances, there are often enough intelligent non-Whites and enough stupid Whites to make the advancement of IQ-based arguments too complex for many individuals to appreciate.

Additionally, most reasonable people will take an inherent dislike to any notion of "inferiority" or "superiority" on moral grounds alone, and so this is not an argument which should be used.

Voting patterns will not be broken by 'racist' arguments, but all indications are that Europeans—and all other peoples—will happily grasp any opportunity to associate on an ethno-centric basis if this can be done without giving offence to other groups or races.

It is our duty to ensure that they have this opportunity.

Appendix 2: The Colonisation of Britain: White British School Pupils Set to be Minority by 2021

An analysis of official Government figures have shown that the ethnic "minority" school-going population will be an absolute majority in British schools by 2021, less than ten years away.

The shocking figures are based on statistics released by the Department for Children, Schools and Families in 2006, which do not take into account the massive flood of immigrants over the previous five years which will skew the time scale further against the indigenous population.

According to the figures, in 2007 at least at least 20 percent of all children in Britain were from the ethnic "minorities" (Graeme Paton, Education Editor, 2, One fifth of children from ethnic minorities, *The Telegraph,* 7 Sep 2007).

The official figures for 2006 showed that ethnic "minorities" accounted for 22 percent of pupils at primary school. This was an increase of 2 percent from the previous year (ibid.).

The 2 percent per year increase in ethnic "minority" pupils was replicated at secondary level schools, which in 2006 rose to 17.7 percent (ibid.).

Discounting increased immigration and using a straight 2 percent growth rate per year, the 2006 figures mean that this year (2010) some 32 percent of all primary school pupils are of ethnic "minority" origin.

Using the same calculation of a 2 percent growth rate, the 2006 figures mean that the 2010 secondary school ethnic "minority" pupil rate stood at 27 percent.

Given this growth rate, white British children will become an absolute minority in British schools by the year 2021, when the "ethnic "minority" levels will reach over 50 percent.

It is important to bear in mind that the 2006 figures are already half a decade old, and do not account for the dramatic increase in immigration over the past five years.

In many areas, white children are already a minority. According to the Birmingham City Council, 61 percent of all primary school children in greater Birmingham this year are already of Third World origin. (Paul Dale, 'Asian pupils outnumber white children in Birmingham primary schools for the first time,' *Birmingham Mail*, 26 January 2010).

In 2007 it was reported that whites were already a minority in London classrooms ((Dominic Hayes, 'UK whites a minority in London classrooms,' *Evening Standard*, 28 Sep 2007) and in 2008, more than 30 state schools in England were made up solely of ethnic minority pupils with no white children on the roll. (Julie Henry, Education Correspondent, Schools made up of only ethnic minorities,' *The Telegraph*, 04 May 2008).

According to data collected by the Office for National Statistics (ONS) between 1992-1994 and 1997-1999, the number of people from "minority" ethnic groups grew by 15 percent compared to 1 percent for white people. ('Ethnic birth rate climbs,' *BBC News* website, 21 September, 2001).

Figures released by the ONS in January 2009 revealed that the Muslim population in Britain has grown by more than 500,000 to 2.4 million in just four years. Their population multiplied 10 times faster than the rest of society. (Richard Kerbaj, 'Muslim population rising 10 times faster than rest of society,' *The Times*, January 30, 2009).

The massive increase in immigration between the years 2006 and 2010 will only have increased the ethnic "minority" population even further, so even the projection of 2021 is possibly "optimistic" and whites will become a minority even before that year.

Appendix 3: Invasion: Immigration Wave Means 650 New UK Citizens Every Day

More than 650 people — mostly from the Third World — are given British citizenship every day in a process which, left unchecked, will see the indigenous population overrun and exterminated within 50 years.

According to immigration statistics released by the Office for National Statistics, some 237,890 people were granted settlement in the Britain in 2010.

This equates to a rise of 22 percent compared with the 194,780 in the previous calendar year and equivalent to more than 650 a day.

Other figures showed that India was the country of birth for the largest number of foreign people arriving in Britain in the 12 months to June 2010, making up about 678,000 of the total.

The second highest number came from Poland (520,000), followed by Pakistan (421,000) and the Republic of Ireland (398,000).

EU rules dictate that Poland has free access to Britain, while historical ties between this country and Ireland also guarantee freedom of movement.

The number of foreigners who left Britain, either voluntarily or through enforced removals, fell to 57,085, the lowest in five years. The number of asylum seekers granted settlement increased to 5,125. This is not however the total number of asylum seekers who arrived in the year under study. Tens of thousands of asylum seekers arrive every year.

The number of work visas granted rose in 2010 by 4 percent to 84,370 compared with 81,185 the previous year.

Even more disturbingly, a total of 334,815 student visas were issued in 2010.

Immigration think tank Migrationwatch has identified the student visa scam as a major avenue of illegal immigration, as many of these students are enrolled at obviously bogus colleges or just vanish into their 'communities.'

Exit controls were abolished by the Major government and since then there are no formal records of who has left the country.

Appendix 4: German Chancellor's "Multiculturalism Has Failed" Remarks Highlight Danger of "Adapt or Integrate" Mentality

German Chancellor Angela Merkel's comment that multiculturalism in Germany has "utterly failed" has once again highlighted the dangerous ignorance of the "adapt or integrate" mentality which pervades civic nationalist thinking.

Ms Merkel's remarks, made to a meeting of her Christian Democrats Union (CDU) party, were widely misinterpreted by the controlled media as some type of "anti-immigration" outburst.

In reality, it is nothing of the sort. Ms Merkel's comments are actually is a call for even greater integration of immigrants from the Third World, not less.

Ms Merkel has in essence endorsed the "become like us and do not form separate societies" philosophy, which is prevalent in Britain in UKIP and other civic nationalist circles.

This belief, that Third World immigrants can "become" German (or "British") simply by learning the language and not forming separate cultural ghettoes inside European countries, is of course as much of a disaster as the "multi-cultural" approach, and just as deadly.

Both approaches fail to account for the reality that all ethnicities are linked to a specific people, and cannot be "transplanted" like clothes or language by checking through an airport terminal.

It is for example, the uniqueness of the British people, their originating population and their ancestry going back tens of thousands of years which make the people of those islands unique.

In the same way, it is the ancestry, heritage and history of the German people which make them unique. Any attempts to deny this uniqueness by pretending that Third World immigrants can "become" British or German just by learning a language and dressing in a bowler hat or lederhosen, is nonsense, born out of ignorance or maliciousness.

To explain this in a simple way:

- Would an African who learned Mandarin and dressed in Oriental clothes become Chinese?

- Would an Englishman who learned Ngaanyatjarra and who dressed in animal skins become an Australian Aborigine?

- Would a Chinese person who learned Yoruba and dressed in African garb become a Nigerian?

- Would an African who learned Iroquoian and dressed in deerskin and wore a feather hat become a North American Indian?

The answer to all these questions is a resounding no, and only an idiot would even contemplate otherwise.

Yet, the very same people who would deride any of the concepts outlined above, would have the rest of the world believe that Africans, Asians, Chinese and all manner of Third Worlders can suddenly "become" European simply by learning the language and dressing like Europeans.

It is this civic nationalist ideology, also known as "cultural nationalism," which is far more insidious and dangerous to the existence of the native people of Europe than even the obviously failed "multiculturalism" to which Ms Merkel referred.

"Multiculturalism" implied the creation of a society in which each culture was allowed to flourish and exist, supposedly "side-by-side," so that the benefits of diversity" would be enjoyed by all.

Multiculturalism, and its twin ideology of "cultural nationalism" ignores the demographic reality of a higher Third world immigrant birth rate. This will inevitably lead to the overwhelming and destruction of the native peoples of Europe, irrelevant of the language and dress of the conquerors.

The fake "multiculturalism" and "cultural nationalism" ideologies, both rooted in civic nationalism, are the collective death knell of all individual peoples.

Only the sound, logical and natural policy of ethno-nationalism is the only alternative which can guarantee the survival of the native, indigenous European people.

Appendix 5: The Colonisation of Britain: Bradford CoE in Crisis as Muslim Population Skyrockets

The Third World immigrant population is growing 15 times faster than the native white British population and this dramatic demographic shift has plunged many historic Anglican dioceses into a severe crisis which threatens their very existence.

According to reports, the Church of England in Bradford diocese now has twice as many Muslim worshippers as Anglicans, a fact which local church leaders have attributed directly to mass immigration.

Canon Rod Anderson, of St Barnabas Church in Heaton, Bradford, was quoted as saying that during his 16 years at the church, the congregation had diminished from more than 100 on Sundays to between 40 and 60.

"I have seen a demographic shift with a large ethnic Asian influx, which has had a noticeable impact on congregation sizes and the knock-on of this is a downturn in financial fortunes," Canon Anderson said.

A newspaper report quoted an "insider" as saying that the "crisis was particularly acute in parts of the country where population shifts had accelerated a general decline in churchgoing, hitting church collections which feed diocesan coffers.

"Some areas with a high concentration of Muslim migrants have experienced 'white flight' and the Church is struggling to maintain a foothold," the unidentified person was quoted as saying.

An analysis done in 2010 of Office for National Statistics (ONS) figures by Migrationwatch-linked expert David Coleman, Professor of Demography at Oxford University, showed that the

Muslim population in Britain was multiplying 10 times faster than the rest of society.

According to Professor Coleman, the increase was directly attributable to immigration and a higher birth rate.

"The implications are very substantial," Professor Coleman said. "Some of the Muslim population, by no means all of them, are the least socially and economically integrated of any in the United Kingdom ... and the one most associated with political dissatisfaction."

This figure ties in well with earlier ONS projections which showed that the ethnic population of Britain as a whole was growing 15 times faster than the indigenous British population.

ONS data showed that the number of people from "minority ethnic groups" grew by 15 percent compared to 1 percent for white people. Other figures have suggested that there will be more Muslims in Britain's mosques on Fridays than Anglicans in church on Sundays within 10 years.

Nowhere is this better illustrated than in the Diocese of Bradford which covers the city, the western quarter of North Yorkshire and parts of East Lancashire, South-East Cumbria and Leeds.

According to official attendance figures, 'usual' Sunday churchgoing across the diocese's 147 parishes fell from 13,500 in 2000 to 8,700 in 2008.

There are now more than 20,000 regular Muslim worshippers in the town which has an astonishing 80 mosques.

The figures make it clear that simply halting Third World immigration will not be enough to save Britain and preserve its unique identity and culture, but that the immigration tsunami will have to be reversed as well.

Appendix 6: Study Which Claims "5.5 Million Muslims in 20 years" in Britain Is a Gross Underestimate

The January 2011 claim by the American "Pew Center" that there will be 5.5 million Muslims in Britain by 2030 is a gross underestimation and based on a significant and serious calculation error, it has emerged.

The Pew Center, which is a Washington DC-based organisation which specialises in public policy study papers, said that Muslims are expected to account for 8.2 percent of the UK's population in 2030, up from an estimated 4.6 percent in 2010.

According to the Pew Center, in "1990 there were 1.1 million Muslims in Britain, representing two per cent of the population."

It was from this base figure that the Pew Center started its calculations and claimed that some 40 years later, the Muslim population would total some 5.5 million.

Separate studies conducted in January 2008 showed that the Muslim population of Britain was already at least 2.4 million strong (or nearly half the Pew Center's proposed 2030 figure) and that the Muslim population was increasing at a rate ten times faster than any other segment of the population.

Furthermore, the high number of Muslims under the age of four in Britain — 301,000 as of September 2009 — of a total of just over 3.5 million, means that in the younger age groups, Muslims were already ten percent of the population a year ago.

Given these birth rates, census figures and the fact that the Muslim population in 2008 was already 2.4 million, it can easily be seen that the Pew Center's predictions are a hopeless underestimate.

In reality, given the demographic trends already visible in London, Birmingham and Leicester, to name but three cities blighted by Third World colonisation, it is likely that the Muslim population of Britain reached 3 million in 2010.

Given that the birth rate amongst Pakistani women living in Britain is three times higher than among British-born women, the figure of 5.5 million is likely to be reached well before 2020, a full decade short of the Pew Center's predictions.

Mohammed has already been the most common newborn boy's name in Britain for at least two years (although the establishment has tried to lie about this by using different spellings of the name to dilute the total count).

If current immigration and fertility rates continue as they are now, white British people will become an absolute minority by 2066, according to a recent report by Professor David Coleman from Oxford University.

Professor Coleman added that white British people will be a minority in younger age groups "well before that date."

Appendix 7: Is it Multiculturalism Which Has Failed?

In January 2011, French president Nicolas Sarkozy announced that "multiculturalism had failed," echoing David Cameron, German Chancellor Angela Merkel, Australia's former prime minister John Howard and former Spanish prime minister Jose Maria Aznar — but is it multiculturalism which has failed, or rather the entire policy of mass Third World immigration?

Much ado has been made of Mr Cameron's recent announcement in this regard, and he has even been accused of "racism" and "stoking racial tension."

However, a closer analysis of what Mr Cameron — and these other leaders — actually means by their statements reveals that they have not admitted that their policies of flooding European countries with Third World immigrants is wrong.

On the contrary. What Mr Cameron and his ilk actually mean is that their policy of allowing separate cultures and identities to be maintained by immigrant groups after they moved to First World countries, is wrong. In other words, Mr Cameron believes that the problem is that there has not been enough integration, and what is needed is even more mixing.

According to Mr Cameron, the problem only lies in the fact that these immigrants have not been forced to adopt First World culture, and have been allowed to continue with their Third World culture and traditions.

This bizarre worldview is the liberal mindset's latest trick to try and explain why the policy which they have endorsed for the last 50 years — mass Third World immigration — has not led to peace and harmony, but rather social discord and the wholesale importation of Third World poverty, chaos and lately, even terrorism.

In his now 'infamous' speech in Munich last weekend, Mr Cameron claimed that "we must build stronger societies and stronger identities at home. Frankly, we need a lot less of the passive tolerance of recent years and a much more active, muscular liberalism."

According to Mr Cameron, a "passively tolerant society says to its citizens, as long as you obey the law we will just leave you alone. It stands neutral between different values."

And therein lies the rub. The liberal mindset has claimed for the past 50 years that "diversity" would bring harmony and that "multiculturalism" was a good thing which would broaden peoples' worldview and make them more tolerant.

The opposite has of course happened, as racial tensions have spiralled upwards in all First World nations subjected to this insanity.

Now, Mr Cameron has argued, that there must be a change. Immigrants, he said, must be "educated in the elements of a common culture and curriculum. It will also help build stronger pride in local identity, so people feel free to say, 'Yes, I am a Muslim, I am a Hindu, I am Christian, but I am also a Londonder or a Berliner too'. It's that identity, that feeling of belonging in our countries, that I believe is the key to achieving true cohesion."

Mr Cameron is wrong. It is not the lack of a "common identity" which is to blame for the disaster which Britain and other First World nations face.

Rather, it is the policy of mass immigration itself which is the cause of the problem, not the maintenance of separate cultures by immigrant groups.

"Multiculturalism" is, of course, doomed to failure as well.

But this is not, per se, the problem. The real danger facing Britain is not if there is a policy of multiculturalism, but rather if the indigenous European people continue to exist or not.

Multiculturalism is a disaster, but forced integration into a "common culture" which will see the European people extinguished, is a disaster of equally great proportions.

This is the truth, and no amount of chameleon-like distortions by the fraudster establishment politicians can disguise it.

Appendix 8: Cockneys: The First British Group to be Ethnically Cleansed

The Cockney culture and language has been ethnically cleansed from London's East End as mass Third World immigration has pushed white people into minority status and destroyed the world-famous accent.

According to an analysis of demographic figures — which are already several years out of date — white British people make up as less than 40 percent of the population in the areas of London traditionally associated with Cockneys.

Furthermore, the world famous Cockney accent and rhyming slang has already been completely replaced amongst the younger age groups in the region as they form the overwhelming majority of that population.

True Cockney, a dialect more than 500 years old, is now spoken only by the elderly in London and will, a study recently showed, be completely extinct within 30 years. Cockney is being replaced by what is politely called "Multicultural London English" or LME for short. LME is also known as "Jafaican" which is a combination of Jamacian, African and Asian.

Traditionally, people born within earshot of the bells of the church of St. Mary-le-Bow in Cheapside, London, were classified as true Cockneys. The original bells of the church, named the "Bow Bells" after the stone arches, or 'bows,' of a church, called St Mary de Arcubus which was built on the site following the Norman Conquest of 1091.

Richard Wittington became Mayor of London in 1392, and legend has it that he returned to London when he heard the Bow Bells as he was about to leave the city.

One of the earliest written references of the bells dates back to 1469, when it was recorded that they were rung a 9pm every evening. The first written reference to an association between the people living in the area and the bells dates to 1600, when the poem 'The letting of humours blood in the head-vaine' by Samuel Rowland appeared. The line in question read "I scorne ... To let a Bowe-bell Cockney put me downe."

The original bells were destroyed along with the building in the Great Fire of London of 1666, and have been recast twice since then, the last time in 1956.

Apart from the world famous accent, which foreigners still strongly identify with England and London, other aspects of Cockney culture have become icons in their own right.

The 'Pearly Kings and Queens' for example, became tourist attractions. They originated amongst market costermongers who decorated their clothes with pearl buttons to differentiate themselves from regular traders.

The 'kings' were elected from within those traders to protect their rights from marketplace rivals, but by the second half of the 20th century, the Pearly Kings and Queens had assumed a more symbolic and charitable role, devoting their time to raising funds for good works.

Nowadays, Pearly Kings and Queens are increasingly rare sights, even in tourist-drenched London.

Cockney characters were so powerful that they found their way into major entertainment works, varying from 19th century music hall performers such as Marie Lloyd and Albert Chevalier to major fiction works such as Bill Sykes (from Dickens's 'Oliver Twist'), Eliza Doolittle (George Bernard Shaw's 'Pygmalion') and others.

The traditional areas in which the Cockney culture originated was the areas of Bethnal Green, Whitechapel, Hackney (which includes Hoxton and Shoreditch), Blackwall, Bow, Bow Common, Bromley-by-Bow, Cambridge Heath, Canary Wharf, Cubitt Town, Docklands, East Smithfield, Fish Island, Globe Town, Isle of Dogs, Leamouth, Limehouse, Mile End, Millwall, Old Ford, Poplar, Ratcliff, St George in the East, Shadwell, Spitalfields, Stepney, and Wapping.

Almost all of these areas today fall under the reach of the London Borough of Tower Hamlets, which according to the 2001 census, had a white British population of 42.9 percent.

In the intervening ten years, the white British population has dropped dramatically through a process of white flight and mass Third World immigration, with current estimates claiming that whites no make up less than one-third of the population.

According to the study "Multicultural London English: the emergence, acquisition and diffusion of a new variety," by Sociolinguistics Professor Paul Kerswill at Lancaster University, this demographic change will cause the Cockney accent to disappear from London's streets within 30 years.

"Cockney in the East End is now transforming itself into Multicultural London English, a new, melting-pot mixture of all those people living here who learnt English as a second language," Prof Kerswill was quoted as saying.

So ends 500 years of history, culture and tradition: wiped out by less than 30 years of mass immigration. The evidence is clear: mass immigration will lead to the ethnic cleansing of Britain's indigenous peoples.

The Cockney's fate is the same one awaiting all of Britain, and indeed, of Europe, unless the insanity and unfairness of current immigration trends are not only halted, but reversed. May we pray that the Cockneys are the last victims of this evil process.